I AM

Two Of The Most
Powerful Words, For What
You Put After Them
Shapes Your Reality

GARY HENSEL

BALBOA.
PRESS

A DIVISION OF HAY HOUSE

Balboa Press books may be ordered through booksellers or by contacting:

Balboa Press
A Division of Hay House
1663 Liberty Drive
Bloomington, IN 47403
www.balboapress.com
1 (877) 407-4847

Because of the dynamic nature of the Internet, any web addresses or
links contained in this book may have changed since publication and
may no longer be valid. The views expressed in this work are solely those
of the author and do not necessarily reflect the views of the publisher,
and the publisher hereby disclaims any responsibility for them.

The author of this book does not dispense medical advice or prescribe
the use of any technique as a form of treatment for physical, emotional,
or medical problems without the advice of a physician, either directly
or indirectly. The intent of the author is only to offer information
of a general nature to help you in your quest for emotional and
spiritual well-being. In the event you use any of the information in
this book for yourself, which is your constitutional right, the author
and the publisher assume no responsibility for your actions.

Any people depicted in stock imagery provided by Thinkstock are
models, and such images are being used for illustrative purposes only.
Certain stock imagery © Thinkstock.

Print information available on the last page.

ISBN: 978-1-5043-7178-0 (sc)
ISBN: 978-1-5043-7179-7 (hc)
ISBN: 978-1-5043-7190-2 (e)

Library of Congress Control Number: 2016920984

Balboa Press rev. date: 12/29/2016

I Am:
Two of the most powerful words, for what
you put after them shapes your reality.

Dedicated to Virginia,
the master who taught me about love.

I would like to acknowledge all
the great masters and teachers
who have taught me so much.

I stand on their shoulders.

There are no original thoughts.
I am but a creation of souls before me.

We will never understand it all.
Understanding that is the
highest form of knowledge.

Every great teacher has told us
that we are infinitely abundant.
If we come from an abundant
universe and God,
we must be abundant.

God is everything.
God does not lack.
You are of God.
You don't have to lack anything.

A man's character is his statement to the universe.

What you feed will grow:
fear or love,
lack or abundance,
pain or gratitude.

What you can conceive can become real.

If we come from an infinite
and abundant universe,
we must be abundant.

Make your first and last thought of the day one of gratitude.

Move away from thinking in terms of lack.
Attempt to remain in a state of gratitude.

If you are struggling with the
concept of attraction,
think in terms of a state of allowing.

Your feelings are stronger
than your knowledge.

Your talents are gifts from God.
Your utilization of those talents
is your gift back to God.

If you only knew how powerful you are....

The subconscious mind cannot tell the difference between dreams and reality. Visualize your dreams.

You can decide to live an abundant life.

Your body will die.
You will take no possessions with you.
You will leave only the footprint
of the love you created.

Ride out each passion until it
no longer serves you.

To refuse your purpose will only create negative energy within you.

Energy must move.
If need be, it will turn on itself.

We are all wounded.
That is part of the human experience.
You are not alone.

Deep inside you already
know your purpose.

Live your life on purpose.

At your moment of greatest
pain, affirm to yourself,
I need this.

Life is infinite and dynamic,
not finite and static.

As you grow,
those around you may
become uncomfortable.

Many times it takes real pain
to create real growth.

Every journey comes to an end.

Passion is the ember that ignites the soul.

Discontent is the universe
nudging your soul.

Does your path have heart and passion?
If not, choose another path.

The soul needs sunshine and nature
as a plant needs sunshine and water.

Learn to embrace each moment.
This is the very definition of walking grace.

Our imagination is very powerful.
It can imagine great love.
It is also capable of imagining great fear.

It is all an illusion.
The biggest illusion is that
you are controlling it all.

Our past difficulties are all perfection.
They have helped shape
us into who we are.

Time, while not real, is one of
our greatest teachers.

Hard times make us more forgiving,
more empathetic, and more generous.
Hard times teach us to surrender to grace.

The wisdom we gain during
our journeys of life
is a gift we must share.

Fear will push away the very
things you desire.

Money is not evil.
It is just a form of energy.

The hoarding of possessions
will only stagnate energy in your life.

Hoarding is from a mentality of lack.

The way money flows in and out of your life is in direct relationship to your thoughts and peace of mind.

We receive what we feel we deserve.

If you are seeking love, be love.
If you are seeking happiness, be happy.

Are you afraid of failing?
Or are you afraid of succeeding?

Indecision is deciding to fail.

Your life is always the present moment.

Stress is caused by wanting
to be in the future
instead of in the now.

Accept the present moment as perfect,
and transform your life.

Feelings do not control you.
They are just feelings.
Let them pass through.

For every illness, wrong, setback, and heartbreak, ask yourself, *what opportunity does this create?* Then you will find the gift.

One of the basic laws of the universe is that like attracts like.
Like energy attracts like energy.

There are two prime energies
in the universe:
love and fear.

To lose confidence in yourself
is to deny you are of God.

Forgive others because you love yourself.

A basic component of happiness is deciding who controls your life.

You can remove a lot of anger from your life by not taking things personally.

Embrace solitude.
Wisdom grows in silence.

Possessions do not create wealth.
True wealth comes from not needing them.

Truth knows truth.

You will never figure it all out.
Stop trying and just *be.*

Don't let the closing door distract you from the one opening.

Everything is born and dying
at the same time.

Change is a universal law.
Let go and embrace it.

Allow and pursue constant
change to awaken
the God-force within you.

Still your mind and master your world.

If it does not create and support growth,
do not defend it.

The expanded mind will not contract.

We are lifetime students.
There is basic joy in learning.

Healing is not always on our timetable,
but healing can create
opportunity for growth.

We always feel we are living in
the most important time.
That is just the ego.

It's okay to get what you want from your life.

You create abundant energy
by being grateful.

To be in the flow is to access the God in you.
It is pure wisdom.

The only thing to master is yourself.

Discipline is a practice of self-respect.

Do not try to control the world.
Be in it.

Nothing is absolute.
Opposites can both be true.

Change your beliefs about yourself,
and you will change your life.

Expect and believe to receive.

You are not a body with a soul.
You are a soul with a body.

Your life is the universe experiencing itself.

The fact that you exist is a miracle.
You are proof of miracles.

Intuition is just a conduit of energy.

Rely more on your intuition and
less on rational thought.
You will access more of your higher self.

Intuition is one way to listen to and communicate with your soul.

The eyes project fear, love, and confidence.
A baby or a dog will look you in the eyes.
A man who is controlled by fear will not.

When your thoughts are of lack,
your life will show lack.

Each event of your life can be viewed
as a problem or an opportunity.

Give energy to your passions and purpose.
Push aside things that do not serve them.

People don't really want things.
They want the emotions they
get from having things.

The key to success in most endeavors is simplicity.

Peace comes with the
abandonment of attachment.

It is our own power that most frightens us.

To grow is to live.

Growth is usually preceded by a fall.

Be an expression of your own being.

Leave a mark of love and wisdom
that will outlive your body.

A bigger life will create bigger peaks and valleys.

You do not have to do or be anything.
You just have to be you, fearlessly.

The true self is revealed in times of crisis.

You do not have to be the most
courageous person.
Just be courageous enough for today.

You become like the people with
whom you surround yourself.

What lies within you is the most powerful force in the universe.

Your character is spoken each
day by the life you live.

Character comes from the French word *caractère,* which means *imprint on the soul.*

Each of us carries baggage.
Ask yourself which bag, if any,
you need to carry farther.

The most powerful human needs are for love, hope, and purpose.

When you are in the flow of life, you expand into pure universal energy.

A troubled past can only be remedied by living in the present.

If is a product of the past and perhaps a lesson to learn, but it is not a place to live.

Your purpose is not to find yourself but to be yourself.

Your life starts anew each moment.

Let the present moment just be.
Accept it and embrace it.

When we worry or think compulsively,
we avoid the present moment.

If we perceive the world as hostile,
then that is the world we will live in.

It is our mind that creates time so that we can move out of the present.

The universe has no concept of time.
Time is a creation of man.

We spend our lives searching
instead of just being.

Make the commitment, eliminate
the clutter and noise, and
walk through the fire.

Live independently of the
opinions of others.

One person lives ten years.
Another person lives one hundred years.
To the universe, the difference
is but a second.

Play a sport or game as if you
have nothing to lose.
Only then will you master it.

We are all replaceable.
Life will go on without us.
When you understand that,
you can start to live.

You have the power to decide the meaning of each event in your life.

We are defined by the stories
we tell about ourselves.
What is the story you tell?

The gentle man has great strength.
The weakest men are cruel.

Time reveals truth.

Make an honest declaration of who you are.
Be proud of it.
Live it.

People want to be heard more than they want to hear advice.

Every human seeks happiness.
We just search for it uniquely.

Education can be expensive in many ways, but a lack of education is even costlier.

Every person in your life is
one of your teachers.

We call to ourselves the lessons we need.

If a perceived negative is lingering in your life, it is probably a needed lesson.

When you can see your failures as a preparation, you have already succeeded.

You are the sum of every person you have interacted with in your life.

Just because the path is well worn
does not mean it is your path.

Your belief in the outcome is the single most important variable and predictor of success.

Your life is the product of all your thoughts.
Hence, your thoughts will
create your future.

Your parents and surroundings may have made an imprint on your early thoughts, but you decide in each moment what your life will be now.

Universal laws:
We are all one.
Our thoughts create.
The source is love.

Live.
Learn.
Share.
Repeat.

Experiencing creates knowing.
Knowing creates wisdom.

All the great teachers, masters, and thinkers across time have been communicating the same messages.

Start saying yes more than you say no,
and life will start saying yes to you.

We have been given life, but we must choose to be alive.

Life is a mystery, and that
creates the wonder.
If you had all the answers, there would
be no reason or need to experience it.

Every relationship teaches us
something about ourselves.

Confrontation fuels the ego.
If you are in an unbalanced relationship,
bless it and move from it.

To feel you are a victim is both a delusion of your ego and a refusal to acknowledge your own power.

The toxic person in your life is your teacher. Ask yourself what you are supposed to learn.

Be willing to let people go.
You are doing them and yourself a favor.
There will be new people who enter
your life, as life itself is abundant.

You make an imprint on people
by how you make them feel.

Remember, this is all a dream.
When you start to believe it is real,
your ego has overtaken your source.

Bless the problem people in your life.
You will remove their power
and empower yourself.

Optimism and pessimism, fear
and faith are all created in your
thoughts, which you control.

Feelings of anxiety, shame, and judgment
create low vibrational energy.
This moves you away from the source.

Belief in limitation gives
energy to limitation.

As sunlight energizes and cleanses,
awareness dissolves fears.

The sun never says to the
earth "You owe me."
Pure love is not conditional.

Three magic words are *acceptance, love,* and *gratitude.*

Fear just means that for a few moments
you have forgotten that you are of
God and that you are perfection.

Lean away from the noise in your head, and let fear pass through you.

Caution in the face of danger is sometimes required, but fear is a choice.

Lose your mind and gain yourself.

Expectancy is a core ingredient of miracles.

Coincidence and synchronicity are the universe speaking to you.

Each moment, you are either
growing or dying.
It is a core of nature.
It's your choice.

The definition of God is that moment in life when everything feels like pure joy and love.

When you choose to feel good, you
are choosing your higher self.
You are choosing God.

Letting go means trusting
in your own divinity.

The miracles you see every day help you believe in the miracles yet to come.

God is not a being.
God is a state of being.

You are but a drop in the universe.
But without your drop, there
would be no universe.

The *doing* is not as important or as powerful as the *being.*

The scarecrow already had a brain,
the lion already had courage, and
the tin man already had a heart.
You already have all you need inside you.

Newton's third law:
For every action there is an equal
and opposite reaction.

You are pure energy.
The death of the body is just a
change in the form of that energy.

You are everything, and you are nothing. Quantum physics tells us that inside the smallest-known particle is nothing.

Your soul is the strongest and
purest form of energy.

Movement creates movement.
Hence, if you want change, then
you must become the change.

You can only receive what you give and are willing to receive back.

Matter is only energy whose vibration has been lowered to create perception.

Just as you can create a positive vibration
of energy, you can create negative
energy with your thoughts and actions,
thus creating the world you live in.

People around you create energy.
You can accept it, repel it, or
move away from it.

Energy is always moving,
changing, and learning.

Your evolutionary process is dominated by your ability to recognize and control the flow of energy around you.

The axiom that water seeks its own level is in the concept that like energy attracts like energy.

If you do not follow your inner guidance,
you will feel emptiness and a loss of energy.

Sometimes the most powerful thing you can do is send out thoughts of positive energy and love to a person.

The most important gift you can give people is to tell them that you love them.

Your thoughts create energy, and
your body carries the energy. Thus,
the energy becomes your life.

You cannot give or receive love if you do not feel love for yourself.

Relationships are merely life experiencing itself.

You become smaller by what you let annoy you, and you become larger by what you let love you.

Your body will fall away, but your
love will endure infinitely.

Love is not a luxury.
It is a necessity for your survival.

The *universe, God,* and *love* are all words with the same meaning.

To find love, do not seek it.
Just be love.
You will not find what you are not.

Learning has a beginning but should never have an ending.

The Tao means a way or path and
is the essence of the universe.

Create calm within, and the world around you will become calm.

Worrying creates unnecessary suffering when the event does not happen, and it doubles the suffering if it does.

Sometimes you have to lose
everything to gain yourself.

We seek security, but letting
go is what gives us peace.

Fear is just misdirected energy.

Stalling the greatness within will only lead to sickness on the outside.

What you fear defines you.

You dishonor God and the universe
when you feel unworthy.

Look for the good.
Embrace it and celebrate it.
As you do, it will expand in your life.

Manifesting is the realization
of what already exists.
We are not creating as much
as we are unveiling.

Effort is merely transferring thought and feeling into action.

Manifestation is not magic.
It is a principle of the universe.
All that you can see started
out as a thought.

To teach is to release potential.

Reality does not make you
feel a certain way.
Your feelings create the reality
you're experiencing.

Like attracts like, spirit recognizes spirit, and love repels fears.

As we reach for and become our higher selves, we leave behind anger, addictions, ego, and fear.

Happiness flows when we create a sense of gratitude, a sense of purpose, and a sense of being present.

When we embrace death as a present,
then we can embrace life in the present.

As you move toward your passions, you demonstrate your intentions to the universe.

Anger leads to disease of the soul
and eventually of the body.

The sweat from your clinging hands will only take from you what you seek.

Release the concept of controlling
your world, and just be your world.

Every journey has a time and a purpose.
When the journey ends, it's
a sign of growth.
Then the next journey begins.

Remove the thought that things and people in your life need fixing.

We attract what we feel worthy of.

Each one of your thoughts
and actions is a prayer.
And your prayers are being answered.

The pessimist will say the optimist is the dreamer. This isn't such a harsh criticism when you consider that it's coming from a source of fear, worry, and negativity.

The most powerful healing
force is within you.

Whether you call it *karma, serendipity,* or *reciprocity,* energy is as energy does. As you move in the direction of your dreams, the right people, books, and funds will appear before you.

You create an energy frequency.
And you have the power to match that
frequency with your intention.

First believe it.
Then you will see it.

Awake each morning with a
thought of intention.
What kind of day and life will you create?

Thought is energy.
Mental images are concentrated energy.
Thought concentrated on defined
intention is powerful.

Do not get lost in the dream.
Experience the human condition while
fulfilling the destiny of your soul.

Nothing in and of itself is good or bad.
Your thoughts create the judgment.

The greatest capital of any organization lies in the thoughts of the people who are in it.

The best way to learn is to teach.

Quantum physics tells us that the observer affects the observation.

The most desirable characteristic of a man is to be open to knowledge.

You ultimately become the books you read and the people with whom you surround yourself.

All paths potentially serve as roads to personal growth.

Your life will have cycles and seasons.
Look to nature as an example.

Mental thought of intention with physical movement in that direction creates manifestation of reality.

Affirmations become belief.
Belief becomes conviction.
Convictions become passion.
Passion creates reality.

All form is condensed emptiness.
Form is merely energy.

Your life will expand or contract in direct correlation with your thoughts about yourself.

Problems are just you experiencing life.
Your ego is looking for ammunition,
and your soul is yearning for growth.

The log in the fireplace must burn to create energy, as must you to create light.

Sometimes you eat the bear.
Sometimes the bear eats you.
It is all the soul experiencing life.

The only real obstacle is yourself.

Life is not a series of problems to be solved but lessons to be learned.

Sometimes it just is.
Suffering is only the refusal to
accept the current reality.

Resist something, and it will cling to you and engulf your life.

Remove the word *should* from your lexicon.
If something serves you,
give it your energy.
If it doesn't, move from it.

Darkness and light define each other.
One cannot exist without the other.

Emotional pain is the ego fighting for life.

One day you will realize the lesson
of whatever stresses you today.

Each storm of your life can either harden your heart or soften your soul.

In moments of challenge or crisis, be still.
Lean away from it.
Let negative thoughts and energy
pass through you and back out.
Return to your source.

We create suffering inside ourselves
when we decide how others should act.
Observe their being, and decide to accept
or move away from their energy.

Your strongest adviser is yourself.

Our true holy wars are within.

Lack of intention results in mere existence.
In each moment, define your intent.

Your intention should not be to
contemplate darkness but to imagine light.

The quality of your thoughts
creates the quality of your life.

You do not arrive at happiness.
You are happiness.

Thinking and viewing life in terms
of problems, lack, and victimhood
can be a powerful addiction.

Most people are desperate, not realizing their own power.

You must declare something before it is so.

What we focus on expands.
Accept full responsibility for your life.

The genius within you is stoked
by the fires of adversity.

Simplicity in life will help you return to the God-like core of your natural being.

Realizing that you need nothing
gives you everything.

There are moments you wish to forget,
but always remember the lesson.
It was a moment and a lesson you needed.

Adversity serves to remind
you who you are.

You are the Holy Grail.

Smother the God within, and you will die. Release it, and you will come to life.

You are not separate from nature.
You are of nature.

The self-righteous are usually self-hating.
One who is truly evolving would take
others with them, not put others down.

The disease of unhappiness is
a symptom of the ego.

The same thought can create heaven or hell, depending on the direction of the energy you give it.

Unhappiness is a byproduct of deciding to be less than what you are meant to be.

Bliss is created when you say
yes to your highest self.

Your job as a parent is to work yourself out of a job.

Align your body and mind with your soul,
and let the ego lose out as often as possible.

There is genius in simplicity.
As you simplify your life, it will get richer.

A choice based on fear will
surrender you of your power.

Indecision is still a choice.

In our darkest moments we must look to see only perfection and express gratitude for it.

Guilty thoughts stagnate growth.
Intelligently reflect, learn, grow,
and decide who you are now.

Worry and fear are prayers.
You are emotionally manifesting
that which you do not want.

First we have rituals with rules, and then we look to science with facts. Then we look within and find ourselves and God.

You are already enough.

Give your energy to improving yourself, not to criticizing others.

Understand that people will try to get you to act in ways that supports their needs.

Always look within.

A master can conquer loneliness and turn solitude into a spiritual experience.

In each moment, be grace.

Dis-ease of the body is a symptom
of a lack of self-love.

All of your work is with self.

You only need to become
what you already are.

Wisdom is the true knowing of the self.

The soul is always speaking to us.
In our darkest hours, we
can hear it the most.

You are a gift to the world.

Become the author of the story of your life.

The word *enthusiasm* translates
to *the God within.*

Surround yourself with people who are vibrating at a high level.

Sensitive people may feel the extremes more because they are more in tune with their souls.

What is within you is more important than what is behind you.

You are responsible for your own joy.

When you stand in your own way,
many obstacles will appear.

We are as perfect as we are flawed.

The center of the world is where you are in this moment.

The only real betrayal is
the betrayal of self.

Eliminate the word *try* from your vocabulary.

The current societal norms do not necessarily create the truth of mankind.

Forget about what you cannot
do at the moment.
Focus on what you *can* do.

People will show you who they are.
Pay attention and believe
what you observe.

Give yourself permission to think for yourself and have your own dreams.

Learn to trust your natural instincts.
They are powerful.

Your life must have meaning.
If you have no profound
purpose, you are dying.

A synonym for God is *love.*

If you believe you are of God, then you will believe your dreams are possible.

One of the most profound spiritual practices is to be with nature.

The great thinkers and masters of humanity have shared abundant wisdom. We only need to be open to it.

Perhaps our greatest fear is our own power.
To accept it requires accountability.

See God in everything, and you will view the world differently.

When you find yourself, you discover God.

A serious pursuit of science will always reveal a universal spirit.

I am certain of nothing.

The universe is abundant.
You are of the universe.
You are abundant.
There is no lack.

The most powerful thought
is one of gratitude.

Now is the only thing that is real.

You are the present moment.
Your life is the quality of that moment.

Change your words and you
will change your thoughts.
Change your thoughts and you
will change your life.

Like attracts like.
Energy attracts energy.
Love attracts love.

The fact that you *are* is a miracle, and it is your birthright to create miracles.

The more painful the hurt, the more powerful the lesson.

The greatest developments of the future
will be human, not technological.

In the end, isn't everything spiritual?

The Lost Soul

The soul is lost when our consciousness
is focused on body and ego.
It is lost in the dream.
The universe is experiencing being human.
But we have forgotten we are
creating the illusion.
We only need to be reminded
that we are of God.
The dream seems so real.
The human illusion is finite.
The soul and the universe are infinite.

Made in the USA
Lexington, KY
15 December 2017